YOUR KNOWLEDGE H

Belal Kayumi

PESTEL Analysis for Turkey

GRIN Verlag

Bibliografische Information der Deutschen Nationalbibliothek:

Die Deutsche Bibliothek verzeichnet diese Publikation in der Deutschen National-
bibliografie; detaillierte bibliografische Daten sind im Internet über http://dnb.d-
nb.de/ abrufbar.

Imprint:

Copyright © 2014 GRIN Verlag GmbH
Druck und Bindung: Books on Demand GmbH, Norderstedt Germany
ISBN: 978-3-656-63272-6

This book at GRIN:

http://www.grin.com/en/e-book/271183/pestel-analysis-for-turkey

GRIN - Your knowledge has value

Der GRIN Verlag publiziert seit 1998 wissenschaftliche Arbeiten von Studenten, Hochschullehrern und anderen Akademikern als eBook und gedrucktes Buch. Die Verlagswebsite www.grin.com ist die ideale Plattform zur Veröffentlichung von Hausarbeiten, Abschlussarbeiten, wissenschaftlichen Aufsätzen, Dissertationen und Fachbüchern.

Visit us on the internet:

http://www.grin.com/

http://www.facebook.com/grincom

http://www.twitter.com/grin_com

University of Applied Sciences and Arts

Hannover

Faculty of Business Administration

Class: Global Perspectives of International Management

Scientific Paper

PESTEL Analysis for Turkey

Author: Belal Kayumi

Year: 2014

Table of contents

Table of figures

List of abbreviations

AKP	Adalet ve Kalkınma Partisi
BIP	Bipolarization, inequality and Polarization
FDI	Foreign Direct Investment
GDP	Gross domestic product
PKK	Partiya Karkerên Kurdistan
UNFCCC	The United Nations Framework Convention on Climate Change

Abstract

Author: Belal Kayumi

Title: PESTEL analysis for Turkey

This scientific paper is written within the scope of the Global Perspectives of International Management. A PESTEL analysis is carried out for Turkey and described with the help of its six factors. In the beginning, the concept PESTEL is explained and later applied to 'Turkey' as a practical example.

1. Introduction

This scientific paper would help investors who are considering an investment in Turkey.

It gives investors an insight into political, economic, social, technological and legislative situation in Turkey which is necessary to invest successfully in the market. With the help of PESTEL analysis, six areas have been analysed and evaluated. In the beginning of this scientific paper, the PESTEL theory is demonstrated and the basic principle of the analysis method is made clear.

Afterwards, the PESTEL analysis is applied to the current situation of Turkey with the help of six factors.

In the end, a conclusion is drawn for investors.

The data in this scientific paper has been lifted mainly from the Internet.

2. Basic principle of the PESTEL analysis

The PESTEL analysis is a procedure which is applied particularly in the areas of marketing, management and strategic controlling.

With the help of suitable illustrations, the analysis method differentiates the six factors or components of PESTEL.

The range of application of the PESTEL analysis covers not only the analysis of companies or organizations, but also the analysis of countries with the help of the six factors. This is most important for investors as it gives a sort of overview of a country covering all the six spheres.

The political factor emphasize the role of the state, the economic factor refers to macro- economic aspects like exchange rates, commercial cycles and different economic growth rates. Among the rest, social influence change cultures and demography, for instance the population will be older and older in many western countries. Technological factors refer to innovations, for example, the Internet and the nanotechnology. The environmental factors deal, for example, with the environmental pollution and the juridical aspects refer to laws, as for example laws of coalescences or laws for society foundations.[1]

As already mentioned, each letter of the word 'PESTEL' stands for six factors of the PESTEL analysis: P stands for Political, E stands for Economic, S for Social system, T for Technology, E for Environmental and L for Legal.

Each factor is analysed with the help of the PESTEL method.

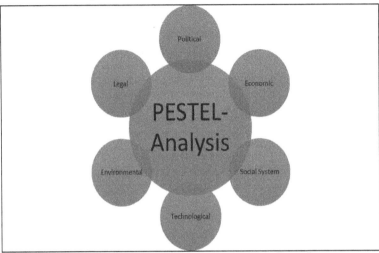

Figure 1: Six factors of Pestel- Analysis Souce: Advisory Council

3. PESTEL analysis for Turkey

In this section, the Pestel analysis is applied to Turkey.

3.1 Political

The basis of Turkish political system is the third Turkish constitution which was framed in 1982. The form of government is parliamentary republic.

In 1996, Turkey made an agreement with the trade union which permitted many Turkish companies to operate successfully in the global economy.

The party AKP which has been ruling since 2002 for justice and development is politically under fire. The AKP has been accused of Islamization of the society.[2]

---

[1] Cf. Johnson/ Scholes/ Whittington 2011, pg. 80f

The government is also rocked by a corruption scandal which deepened the political crisis.[3]

Terrorist organizations like PKK also put the country under threat. Repeated terror attacks shattered Turkey. Turkish soldiers had been deployed frequently to bring the situation under control.[4] Therefore, terrorists' threat is a big disadvantage for a company that wants to set up business in the country.

However, exports rose by 10% on average over the last years. In 2012, the total exports of Turkey amounted to $151.9 billion.[5]

3.2 Economic

Turkey is mainly a free market economy[6]. Non-achievers/weaker citizens do not have same chances in a fiercely competitive free market economy. Therefore, the free market economy is often criticized because of the country's support for the achievement-seekers.

One of the economic strengths of Turkey is the foreign direct investments (FDI). According to A. T. Kearney, Turkey ranks the 13th most attractive location worldwide under the foreign direct investments index.

By the end of 2011, as many as 30,000 enterprises with foreign capital were active in Turkey.[7]

The majority of the foreign direct investments come from the EU, North America and the Gulf States.[8]

The FDI inflows, however, are invested for the development of the country's infrastructure.[9]

For German investors and exporters, there are opportunities in the energy sector (also renewable energy). Opportunities are also there in the field of infrastructure, tourism and in the protection of environment. However, rising

---

[2] Frankfurter Allgemeine (2014)
[3] Spiegel Online (2014)
[4] BBC (2014)
[5] Invest in Turkey (2013a)
[6] CIA- The World Factbook(2013a)
[7] Invest in Turkey (2013b)
[8] Invest in Turkey (2013c)
[9] BVL- Bundesvereinigung (2014a)

labour costs and persistent tax load put modernization of Turkish industrial companies under pressure. [10]

The GDP currently amounts to $789.3 billion and the GDP growth stands at 2.2%. The service industry (62.9%), the industrial sector (28.6%) and the agriculture sector contribute to influence the BIP. [11]

The present inflation rate as seen in the graph stands at 6.54%.[12]

The line graph shows the inflation rate of the last years in Turkey. The inflation rate fell drastically as the International Monetary Fund released a loan of $476 million to Turkey on the one hand and, on the other hand, the debt repayments which would have been due in 2004 and 2005 were shifted to 2006.[13] The inflation rate, however, remains stable in the healthy area.

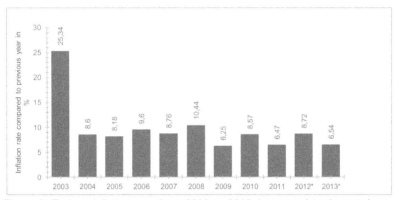

Figure 2: Turkey: Inflation rate from 2003 to 2013 (compared to the previous year) Source: Statista Inc.

In comparison to the G-20 states, Turkey's balance of payments deficit is highest. In January, the difference between exports and imports stands at $6 million. The higher credit grants and the dependence on energy imports are the two main reasons for the highest balance of payments deficit.[14]

[10] BVL- Bundesvereinigung Logistik (2014b)
[11] The World Bank (2014)
[12] Statista (2014)
[13] International Monetary Fund (2014)
[14] DEUTSCH TÜRKISCHE NACHRICHTEN (2014a)

3.3 Social

One of the biggest advantages of Turkey is its demographic profile. More than half of the population is under 30 years. This means the country has a huge potential for productive employees. This young generation offers the spirit of enterprise to speed up the country's growth. The following graph makes this amply clear.

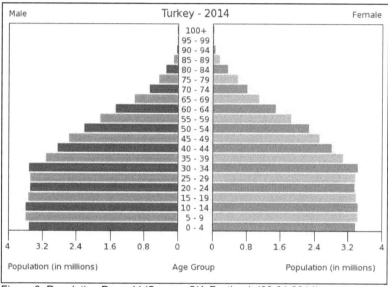

Figure 3: Population Pyramid (Source: CIA Factbook (28.01.2014))

In comparison to the European countries, for example, Germany or France, where the demographic profile is marked by an older population, the Turkish population is clearly younger.[15]

However, one of the disadvantages is high unemployment rate in Turkey. The young unemployment relating to different aspects of labour market poses a big problem. Currently, the rate of unemployment is 9.1%.[16]

---

[15] CIA- The World Factbook (2013b)
[16] Eurostat (2013)

The companies who would like to invest in Turkey would have to bear in mind these challenges and position themselves accordingly.

3.4 Technological

Turkey, according to an article, offers one of the strongest markets for technologies in the world. The use of Internet plays an important role. According to gemalto.com, 78% of the population use Internet regularly. However, Turkey has not yet reached the peak of development in this area. Internet plays a significant role not only for young people, but also for big companies and the Turkish government.

Besides, Turkey has been the first country which allowed the transfer without bank map. It has introduced the NFC (mobile Near-Field Communications) or the eID (electronic identification maps).

Particularly in the areas of Transfer, identity and authentication, Turkey is ahead of its western neighbours by some years.[17] This aspect can be a big competitive advantage for investment in Turkey for the future.

In the area of nanotechnology, the country has made significant progress. Engineers developed in Turkey are made up of new material using nanotechnology. This new material could also be used in satellite. The project is financed by the TÜBITAK of the Turkish institution for scientific and technological research (Türkiye Bilimsel ve Teknolojik Araştırma Kurumu).

Turkey becomes the first country in the world which uses this new material in space. [18]

Germany belongs to the prominent cooperation partners.[19]

Turkey has also built the new centre for nanotechnology (UNAM the Turkish national research centre).

Another interesting thing is the Marmaray tunnel, a Turkish-Japanese project which costs 5 million euros[20]. On September 29, 2013, Turkey initiated the first transcontinental tunnel of the world. The 62-metre-deep tunnel is the deepest tunnel of the world. The major task of the tunnel is to connect the Asian part

---

[17] DEUTSCH TÜRKISCHE NACHRICHTEN (2013b)
[18] Short News (2013)
[19] DEUTSCH TÜRKISCHE NACHRICHTEN (2013c)
[20] Marmaray (2003):

with the European part of Istanbul. The tunnel is 13.6 km long and should be able to transport approximately 75,000 people an hour. Moreover, the tunnel would be built in such a way so that it can withstand an earthquake of 7.5 magnitude.[21] In the future, Turkey plans to construct a car tunnel and the biggest airport of the world, according to an article published in *Time*.

3.5 Environmental

Turkey has natural resources like coal, minerals, oil and petrol.

Today Turkey is the most important supplier of these resources across the world. With the export of granite, basalt and kaolin, the country asserts itself as a competitor in international trade.

However, Turkey imports minerals magnesite, feldspar, Perlite, Bentonite, Dolomite and metals like gold, lead, copper, chrome and silver. The mineral resources lie in the southwest zone of Turkey.[22]

However, despite adopting the methods of modernization, the Turkish mining lacks innovation, suffers from sluggishness and lack of proper investments. So, Turkey cannot utilize its resources to its full potential. Particularly, the mineral resources in Anatolia have not been explored properly. In the area of environment protection, Turkey tries to follow the example of the EU. In 2004, Turkey signed with UNFCCC and has the strong growth with the fall in greenhouse gas emission.[23]

The principal energy source of the country is coal. Therefore, it has a strong environmental impact on Turkey.[24] To combat the environmental pollution, a Turkish-German fermentation gas project was set up. This climate-friendly project uses agricultural rubbish as raw material where resources are used optimally to generate renewable energy. [25]

Environment poses a big disadvantage for companies and investors. Since many customers put more value on environmentally-friendly products, this can lead to the fact that products made in Turkey may not sell.

---

[21] Die Welt (2014)
[22] CIA- The World Factbook (2013c)
[23] United Nations Framework Convention on Climate Change (2013)
[24] Sourcewatch (2013)
[25] Bueroberg

The threat of a severe earthquake also looms over Turkey.

In the last few years, there were earthquake again and again, for example in Analya, the 28th December last year with a magnitude of 2.9. The newspaper 'Die WELT' reported that an extremely dangerous seismic focus only 20 km from Istanbul was identified. Such a natural disaster will lead to immense destructions.

Therefore, there is a disadvantage for a company to set up a plant in Turkey.

3.6 Legal

The Turkish code of commercial law has lot of resemblances to the German German Commercial Code. Turkish companies are comparable with German companies.

However, all laws of the different types of company are standardized in the code of commercial law unlike in Germany where special laws are in vogue for different types of company, for example, the laws for the German Ltd.

The Turkish Limited (Ltd) and the public limited company are the most important types of company in operation.

3.6.1 Turkish Limited (Limited Sirketi)

One finds conditions for setting up the Turkish Limited in the article 503 ff. (old version) and in the article. 573 573 ff. (new version). After the revised version, the setting up of the Turkish Limited by an individual is possible according to article 574 (new version).

All related writing for Turkish limited must be notary accredited social contract as per article 575 (new version).. The social contract must contain certain specifications for the joint stock.

This is explained in greater detail in the article. 506 (new version).. and article 576 (new version).

According to the article, 580 par.1 (new version), the minimum joint stock with the Turkish Limited amounts to 10,000 TL.[26] This corresponds to approx. 3.265

---

[26] The Turkish code of commercial law (2013)

euros. As per article 585 (new version), this must be inserted immediately and in complete detail.[27]

Afterwards, it is registered as the Turkish Limited in the Turkish trade register (ticaret sicili) and is announced in the Turkish trade register sheet. Only after the registration, the Turkish Limited becomes legally responsible as per article 512 (new version).

The German Ltd supports the Turkish Limited only with its company property as it does in Germany, i.e. there is no personal liability of the company member, according to article 602 (new version).

Will represent the type of company by her manager and to the organs of the Turkish Limited company meeting (Genel Kurul), article belong. 616 f. (new version), the manager (Müdürler), article 623 ff. (new version) and the inspector (Denetciler), kind. 635 (new version).[28]

3.6.2 Public limited company in Turkey

Regulations about the public limited company are described in the articles 329-563 (new version).

The public limited company can be set up for economic and legal purpose, according to article 331(new version).

A report on the audit of operating results is also necessary for the setting up of the company. Juridical as well as natural persons can be found in a Turkish public limited company. Even a single individual can set up a public limited company, as per article 338 par. 1 (new version).

The share capital (başlangıç sermayesi) in the type of company amounts to 50,000 TL.[29] This corresponds to approx. 16.328 euros. The general meeting (Genel Kurul), article belong to the organs of the Turkish public limited company. 407 ff. (new version)., the executive board (yönetim kurulu), article. 359 ff. (new version).and as well as in the Turkish Limited of the inspector (denetçi), article. 397 ff.[30]

---

[27] The Turkish code of commercial law (2013)
[28] The Turkish code of commercial law (2013)
[29] The Turkish code of commercial law (2013)
[30] The Turkish code of commercial law (2013)

4. Conclusion

The basic principle of the PESTEL analysis has been explained in this scientific paper and later applied to Turkey.

The gathering of data was easy. In a lot of resources from the Internet, information or data were also found with reference to the current situation of the country.

From the management perspective and the six factors of the PESTEL analysis, Turkey has become a stable and promising economy over the last few years. Therefore, an investment would be worthwhile in Turkey especially in the industries, energy and infrastructure sectors.

As already mentioned, Turkey has vast young population compared to the EU countries and it can offer an attractive investment destination with big domestic market, low taxes and incentives for the foreign investors.

However, based on the PESTEL analysis one should look at each factor in greater detail.

Bibliography

BBC (2014)
URL: http://www.bbc.co.uk/news/world-europe-19650034
[Date: 20.01.2014]

Bueroberg
URL: http://www.bueroberg.com/newsletter/biogasjournal_suluova.pdf
[Date: 25.12.2013]

BVL- Bundesvereinigung Logistik (2014a)
URL: http://www.bvl.de/tuerkei [Date: 10.01.2014]

BVL- Bundesvereinigung Logistik (2014b)
URL: http://www.bvl.de/tuerkei [Date: 10.01.2014]

CIA- The World Factbook (2013a)
URL: https://www.cia.gov/library/publications/the-world-factbook/geos/tu.html
[Date: 25.12.2013]

CIA – The World Factbook (2014b): Turkey [Online]
URL: https://www.cia.gov/library/publications/the-world-factbook/geos/tu.html
[Date: 31.12.13]

CIA- The World Factbook (2013c)
URL: https://www.cia.gov/library/publications/the-world-factbook/fields/2111.html [Date: 31.12.2013]

Das Portal zu Recht & Wirtschaft der Türkei (2013): The Turkish code of commercial law
URL: http://www.tuerkei-recht.de/recht-und-gesetz-allgemein/gesetze/index.php
[Date: 15.01.2014]

DEUTSCH TÜRKISCHE NACHRICHTEN (2013a):Türkei- Höchstes
Leistungsbilanzdefizit aller G-20 Staaten
URL: http://www.deutsch-tuerkische-nachrichten.de/2012/03/426032/tuerkei-
hoechstes-leistungsbilanzdefizit-aller-g-20-staaten-2/
[Date: 17.12.2013]

DEUTSCH TÜRKISCHE NACHRICHTEN(2013b):
URL: http://www.deutsch-tuerkische-nachrichten.de/2012/01/351840/internet-
zeitalter-tuerkei-ist-den-westlichen-laendern-um-jahre-voraus/
[Date: 18.01.2014]

DEUTSCH TURKISCHE NACHRICHTEN(2013c): Forschung und Entwicklung:
Deutschland und Türkei sind enge Kooperations-Partner
URL: http://www.deutsch-tuerkische-nachrichten.de/2013/11/493307/forschung-
und-entwicklung-deutschland-und-tuerkei-sind-enge-kooperations-partner/
[Date: 18.01.2014]

Die Welt: Neuer Megatunnel verbindet Europa und Asien
URL: http://www.welt.de/reise/Fern/article121319945/Neuer-Mega-Tunnel-
verbindet-Europa-und-Asien.html [Date: 19.01.2014]

Die Welt (29.10.2013):
URL: http://www.welt.de/reise/Fern/article121319945/Neuer-Mega-Tunnel-
verbindet-Europa-und-Asien.html [Date. 31.12.13]

Eurostat (2013)
URL:http://appsso.eurostat.ec.europa.eu/nui/show.do?dataset=ei_lmhr_m&lang
=en [Date: 18.01.2014]

Frankfurter Allgemeine (2014): Islamisierung durch vage Programmatik
URL: http://www.faz.net/aktuell/wissen/wissenschaft/islamisierung-durch-vage-
programmatik-1628127.html
[Date: 20.*01.13]*

International Monetary Fund (2014)

URL:http://www.imf.org/external/np/fin/tad/extforth.aspx?memberKey1=980&dat

e1key=2003-10-

31&category=FORTH&year=2003&trxtype=REPCHG&overforth=F&schedule=o

bl [Date: 20.01.2014]

ISPAT, Invest in Turkey:

URL: http://www.invest.gov.tr/en-US/infocenter/news/Pages/020113-turkey-

2012-exports-hit-record-high.aspx

[Date: 31.12.2013]

ISPAT, Invest in Turkey (2013b):

URL: http://www.invest.gov.tr/en-

US/investmentguide/investorsguide/pages/FDIinTurkey.aspx

[Date: 31.12.2013]

Johnson, G., Scholes, K., Whittington, R., (2011): Strategisches

Management Eine Einführung: Analyse, Entscheidung und Umsetzung,

Pearson Studium, München 2011, pp. 80-81

Marmaray (2003): Technical

URL: http://www.marmaray.com/html/technical.html

[Date: 19.01.2014]

Short News: Türkische Wissenschaftler bringen Nanotechnologie in den

Weltraum

URL: http://www.shortnews.de/id/840239/tuerkische-wissenschaftler-bringen-

die-nanotechnologie-in-den-weltraum

[Date: 18.01.2014]

Sourcewatch (2013)

URL: http://www.sourcewatch.org/index.php/Turkey_and_coal

[Date: 25.12.2013]

Spiegel Online (2011)

URL: http://www.spiegel.de/politik/ausland/korruptionsskandal-in-der-tuerkei-um-recep-tayyip-erdogan-a-940852.html

[Date: 20.01.2014]

Statista (2014)

URL: http://de.statista.com/statistik/daten/studie/216056/umfrage/inflationsrate-in-der-tuerkei/ [Date: 20.01.2014]

United Nations Framework Convention on Climate Change (2013)

URL:http://unfccc.int/files/ghg_emissions_data/application/pdf/tur_ghg_profile.pdf [Date: 25.12.2013]

Zeit Online: Türkei will größten Flughafen der Welt bauen

URL: http://www.zeit.de/wirtschaft/2013-01/flughafen-tuerkei-projekt

[Date: 20.01.2014]

www.ingramcontent.com/pod-product-compliance
Ingram Content Group UK Ltd.
Pitfield, Milton Keynes, MK11 3LW, UK
UKHW041318280225
4808UKWH00017B/95